DRINK
PINK

First published in Great Britain in 2019 by Pyramid,
an imprint of Octopus Publishing Group Ltd
Carmelite House, 50 Victoria Embankment, London EC4Y 0DZ
www.octopusbooks.co.uk

ISBN 978-0-7537-3351-6

A CIP catalogue record for this book is available from the British Library

Printed and bound in China

10 9 8 7 6 5 4 3 2 1

Publisher: Lucy Pessell
Designer: Lisa Layton
Editor: Sarah Vaughan
Production Manager: Lucy Carter

The measure that has been used in the recipes is based on a bar jigger, which is 25 ml (1 fl oz).
If preferred, a different volume can be used, providing the proportions are kept constant within
a drink and suitable adjustments are made to spoon measurements, where they occur.

Standard level spoon measurements are used in all recipes.
1 tablespoon = one 15 ml spoon
1 teaspoon = one 5 ml spoon

This book contains cocktails made with raw or lightly cooked eggs. It is prudent for more
vulnerable people to avoid uncooked or lightly cooked cocktails made with eggs.

Some of this material previously appeared in *Pink Drinks* and *Hamlyn All Colour Cookery:
200 Classic Cocktails*.

DRINK PINK

INTRODUCTION

From the classy blush of the Pink Lady to the
sassy flush of the Cosmopolitan, the
peach-pink perfection of the Bellini to the
flashy-trashy confection of the Valentine
Martini, *Drink Pink* is a collection of classic
and contemporary cocktails in every shade
of pink for every occasion.

CONTENTS

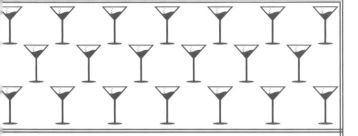

FIZZES,
HIGHBALLS
&
COLLINSES

FRESH PALOMA

½ pink grapefruit, peeled

2 measures blanco tequila

2 measures soda water

1 teaspoon agave syrup

pink grapefruit wedge, to decorate

Juice the pink grapefruit and add the juice to a glass full of ice cubes.

Add the remaining ingredients to the glass, decorate with a grapefruit wedge and serve.

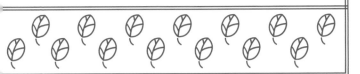

FLORA DORA

½ teaspoon sugar syrup
juice of ½ lime
½ teaspoon grenadine
2 measures gin
dry ginger ale, to top up
lime twist, to decorate

Put 4–5 ice cubes into a cocktail shaker.

Add the sugar syrup, lime juice, grenadine and gin and shake until a frost forms.

Pour without straining into a tall glass.

Top up with dry ginger ale, decorate with a lime twist.

WATERMELON SPRITZ

4 chunks watermelon, plus slice, to decorate

2 measures lemon vodka

2 measures bitter lemon

1 measure apple juice

4 teaspoons lemon juice

3 teaspoons agave syrup

1 sprig mint

2 measures soda water, to top up

Add the watermelon to a cocktail shaker and muddle.

Add the vodka, apple juice, mint, lemon juice and agave syrup.

Shake and strain into a sling glass full of ice cubes and top up with soda water.

Decorate with a watermelon slice and serve.

SEA BREEZE

makes 2

2 measures vodka
4 measures cranberry juice
2 measures grapefruit juice
lime wedges, to decorate

Fill 2 highball glasses with ice cubes, pour over the vodka, cranberry juice and grapefruit juice and stir well.

Decorate with lime wedges and serve.

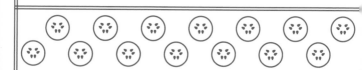

BERRY COLLINS

makes 2

8 raspberries, plus extra to decorate

8 blueberries, plus extra to decorate

1–2 dashes strawberry syrup

4 measures gin

4 teaspoons lemon juice

sugar syrup, to taste

soda water, to top up

lemon slices, to decorate

Muddle the berries and strawberry syrup in the bottom of each glass, then fill each glass with crushed ice.

Add the gin, lemon juice and sugar syrup.

Stir, then top up with the soda water.

Decorate with berries and lemon slices and serve.

BAY BREEZE

makes 2

2 measures vodka
4 measures cranberry juice
2 measures pineapple juice
lime wedges, to decorate

Fill 2 highball glasses with ice cubes, pour over the vodka, cranberry juice and pineapple juice and stir well.

Decorate with lime wedges and serve.

SINGAPORE SLING

makes 2

2 measures gin
1 measure cherry brandy
½ measure Cointreau
½ measure Bénédictine
1 measure grenadine
1 measure lime juice
10 measures pineapple juice
1–2 dashes Angostura bitters

To decorate
pineapple wedges
maraschino cherries

Half-fill a cocktail shaker with ice cubes and put some ice cubes into each highball glass.

Add the remaining ingredients to the shaker and shake until a frost forms on the outside of the shaker.

Strain over the ice cubes into the glasses.

Decorate each one with a pineapple wedge and a maraschino cherry and serve.

PINK COOLER

5 chunks watermelon, plus extra, to decorate

2 measures lemon vodka

2 measures bitter lemon

Add the watermelon to a cocktail shaker and muddle.

Add the vodka and shake.

Strain into a glass full of ice cubes and top up with the bitter lemon.

Decorate with a chunk of watermelon and serve.

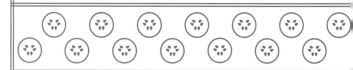

STRAWBERRY FIELDS

1 camomile tea bag
2 measures gin
1 measure strawberry purée
2 teaspoons lemon juice
1 measure double cream
3 teaspoons egg white
3 measures soda water
1 strawberry to decorate

Place the tea bag and gin in a cocktail shaker and leave to infuse for 2 minutes.

Remove the tea bag, add the strawberry purée, lemon juice, double cream and egg white.

Fill the shaker with ice cubes.

Shake and strain into a wine glass and top up with the soda water.

Decorate with a strawberry and serve.

PLAYA DEL MAR

makes 2

2 orange slices

light brown sugar and sea salt, mixed

2½ measures tequila gold

1½ measures Grand Marnier

4 teaspoons lime juice

1½ measures cranberry juice

1½ measures pineapple juice

To decorate

pineapple wedges

orange rind spirals

Frost the rim of each glass by moistening it with an orange slice, then pressing it into the sugar and salt mixture.

Fill each glass with ice cubes.

Pour the tequila, Grand Marnier and fruit juices into a cocktail shaker.

Fill the shaker with ice cubes and shake vigorously for 10 seconds, then strain into the glasses.

Decorate each glass with a pineapple wedge and an orange rind spiral.

BITTER SPRING

1 measure Aperol

2 measures grapefruit juice

4 measures soda water

grapefruit wedge, to decorate

Add the Aperol, grapefruit juice and soda water to wine glass full of ice cubes.

Stir, decorate with a grapefruit wedge and serve.

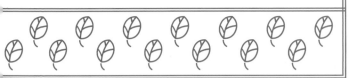

GIN SLING

makes 2

6 measures gin

2 measures cherry
brandy

juice of one lemon

soda water, to top up

Half-fill a cocktail shaker with
ice cubes and put some ice
cubes into 2 highball glasses.

Add the gin, cherry brandy
and lemon to the shaker and
shake until a frost forms on
the outside of the shaker.

Strain over the ice cubes into
the glasses and top up with
soda water.

TIJUANA SLING

1¾ measures tequila gold
¾ measure crème de cassis
¾ measure fresh lime juice
2 dashes of Péychaud bitters
4 measures ginger ale

To decorate
lime wheels
blueberries

Pour the tequila, crème de cassis, lime juice and bitters into a cocktail shaker.

Add some ice cubes and shake vigorously.

Pour into a highball glass then top up with ginger ale.

Decorate with lime wheels and blueberries.

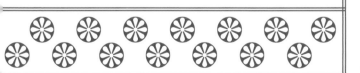

LONG BLUSH

1 measure vodka
2 teaspoons honey
1 measure pomegranate juice
2 teaspoons lime juice
1 measure rosé wine
5 mint leaves
2 measures soda water
mint sprig and pomegranate seeds, to decorate

Add the vodka, honey, pomegranate and lime juices, wine and mint leaves to a cocktail shaker and shake.

Strain into glass and add the soda water.

Top up the glass with crushed ice, decorate with a mint sprig and some pomegranate seeds and serve.

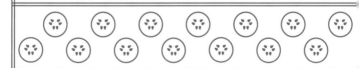

PINK MOJITO

6 mint leaves, plus a sprig to decorate
juice of ½ lime
2 teaspoons sugar syrup
3 raspberries
1½ measures white rum
½ measure Chambord liqueur
cranberry juice, to top up

Muddle the mint, lime juice, sugar syrup and raspberries in a highball glass.

Add some crushed ice and pour in the rum and Chambord.

Stir well, add more ice, top up with cranberry juice and decorate with a mint sprig.

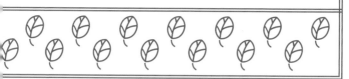

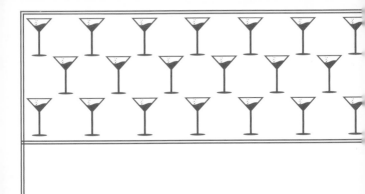

SPIRIT
FORWARDS

BITTERSWEET SYMPHONY

1 measure gin
1 measure Campari
½ measure passion fruit syrup
½ measure fresh lemon juice
lemon slices, to decorate

Put the gin, Campari, passion fruit syrup and lemon juice into a cocktail shaker with some ice cubes and shake to mix.

Strain into an old-fashioned glass over 4–6 ice cubes and decorate with lemon slices.

CHERRY JULEP

juice of ½ lemon
1 teaspoon sugar syrup
1 teaspoon grenadine
1 measure cherry brandy
1 measure sloe gin
2 measures gin
lemon twists, to decorate

Put 3–4 ice cubes into a cocktail shaker.

Pour the lemon juice, sugar syrup, grenadine, cherry brandy, sloe gin and gin over the ice and shake until a frost forms.

Fill a highball glass with finely chopped ice.

Strain the cocktail and pour into the ice-filled glass, decorate with lemon twists and serve.

SPICED BERRY JULEP

1 tablespoon frozen mixed berries, plus extra to decorate

1 measure cinnamon & nutmeg-infused bourbon

6 mint leaves, plus an extra sprig, to decorate

2 teaspoons sugar syrup

Put the berries, bourbon and mint in a glass and muddle.

Leave to stand for 5 minutes, then add the sugar syrup and half fill the glass with crushed ice and churn with the muddler.

When it is thoroughly mixed, top the glass up with crushed ice.

Decorate with frozen berries and serve.

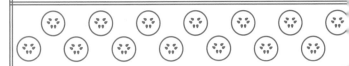

SILK STOCKING

drinking chocolate powder
¾ measure tequila
¾ measure white crème de cacao
4 measures single cream
2 teaspoons grenadine

Dampen the rim of a chilled cocktail glass and dip it into the drinking chocolate powder.

Pour the tequila, white crème de cacao, cream and grenadine into a cocktail shaker and add the ice cubes.

Shake for 10 seconds and strain into the chilled glass.

AUTUMN DAWN

½ measure vodka
½ measure Cointreau
1 teaspoon fresh lemon juice
1 teaspoon Chambord liqueur

Put the vodka, Cointreau and lemon juice into a shaker with some ice cubes and shake briefly.

Strain into a shot glass and carefully drop in the Chambord.

VALENTINE MARTINI

makes 2

4 measures raspberry vodka

12 raspberries, plus extra to decorate

1 measure lime juice

2 dashes sugar syrup

lime rind spirals, to decorate

Half-fill a cocktail shaker with ice cubes.

Add all the remaining ingredients and shake until a frost forms on the outside of the shaker.

Double-strain into 2 chilled martini glasses.

Decorate with raspberries and lime rind spirals on cocktail sticks and serve.

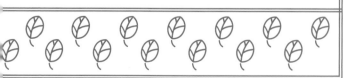

PINK LADY

2½ measures Plymouth gin

1 measure Calvados or
applejack brandy

1 measure fresh lemon juice

½ measure grenadine

1 fresh egg white

stemmed cocktail cherry, to
decorate

Put the gin, Calvados, lemon juice, grenadine and egg white into a cocktail shaker with some ice cubes and shake well, then strain into a chilled cocktail glass.

PINK ANGEL

½ measure white rum
¼ measure advocaat
¼ measure cherry brandy
1 egg white
½ measure double cream

Put some ice cubes into a cocktail shaker with the rum, advocaat, cherry brandy, egg white and cream and shake well.

Strain into a cocktail glass.

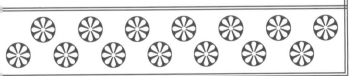

WATERMELON MARTINI

makes 2

3 measures vodka
1 measure passionfruit liqueur
8 chunks watermelon
1 dash cranberry juice
water melon wedges, to
decorate

Put all of the ingredients in
a cocktail shaker.

Add ice cubes and shake.

Strain into 2 chilled martini
glasses and decorate each
glass with a watermelon
wedge.

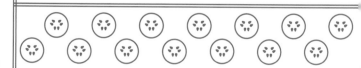

PINK GIN

3–4 dashes angostura bitters
2 meaures gin

Shake the bitters into a glass filled with ice.

Add the gin and stir.

Strain into a chilled cocktail glass.

BELLINI-TINI

2 measures vodka
½ measure peach purée
½ measure peach schnapps
4 drops of peach bitters
2 peach wedges, to decorate

Put some ice cubes into a cocktail shaker, add the vodka, peach purée, peach schnapps and peach bitters and shake well.

Strain into a cocktail glass, decorate with peach wedges.

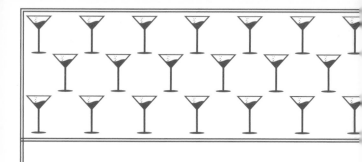

SOURS

STRAWBERRY DAIQUIRI

3 strawberries, hulled

dash of strawberry syrup

6 mint leaves, plus a sprig to decorate

2 measures golden rum

2 measures lime juice

strawberry slice, to decorate

Muddle the strawberries, syrup and mint leaves in the bottom of a cocktail shaker.

Add the rum and lime juice, shake with ice and double-strain into a chilled martini glass.

Decorate with a strawberry slice and a sprig of mint.

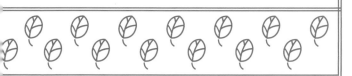

SWALLOW DIVE

1 measure honey vodka

1 measure Chambord

1 measure lime juice

4 raspberries, plus extra to decorate

Put some ice cubes into a cocktail shaker with all the other ingredients. Shake well.

Strain in an old-fashioned glass over crushed ice.

Top up with more crushed ice and decorate with 2 raspberries.

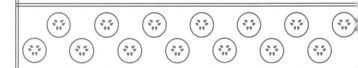

STRAWBERRY & MINT DAIQUIRI

3 strawberries
dash of strawberry syrup
6 mint leaves
2 measures golden rum
1 measure fresh lime juice

To decorate
strawberry slice
mint sprig

Muddle the strawberries, syrup and mint leaves in the bottom of a cocktail shaker.

Add the rum and lime juice, shake with ice cubes and double strain into a chilled cocktail glass.

Decorate with a strawberry slice and a mint sprig.

PINK
CLOVER
CLUB

juice of 1 lime
dash of grenadine
1 egg white
3 measures gin
strawberry slice, to decorate

Put 4–5 ice cubes into a cocktail shaker.

Pour the lime juice, grenadine, egg white and gin over the ice and shake until a frost forms, then strain into a cocktail glass.

Decorate with a strawberry slice.

FRENCH PINK LADY

2 measures gin
4 raspberries
1 measure Triple Sec
3 teaspoons lime juice
1 teaspoon pastis
lime wedge, to decorate

Add the gin, raspberries, Triple Sec, lime juice and pastis to a cocktail shaker and muddle.

Fill the shaker with ice and shake, then strain into a glass.

Decorate with a lime wedge and serve.

VANILLA DAISY

2 measures Bourbon whiskey

1 measure fresh lemon juice

1 measure vanilla syrup

1 teaspoon grenadine

2 cocktail cherries, to decorate

Put the Bourbon, lemon juice and vanilla syrup into a cocktail shaker with some crushed ice and shake well.

Strain into an old-fashioned glass filled with fresh crushed ice then drizzle the grenadine through the drink.

Decorate with cocktail cherries.

PINK COCONUT DAIQUIRI

2 measures white rum
1 measure coconut liqueur
2 measures fresh lime juice
1 teaspoon grenadine
lime slice, to decorate

Put the crushed ice into a cocktail shaker.

Pour the rum, coconut liqueur, lime juice and grenadine over the ice and shake until a frost forms.

Strain into a cocktail glass, decorate with a lime slice.

57

COSMOPOLITAN

1½ measures lemon vodka
4 teaspoons Triple Sec
3 teaspoons lime juice
1 measure cranberry juice
lime wedge, to decorate

Add all the ingredients to a cocktail shaker.

Shake and strain into a glass.

Decorate with a lime wedge and serve.

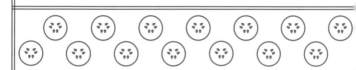

JACK ROSE

2 measures apple brandy
3 teaspoons grenadine
4 teaspoons lemon juice

Add all the ingredients to a cocktail shaker.

Shake, strain into a glass and serve.

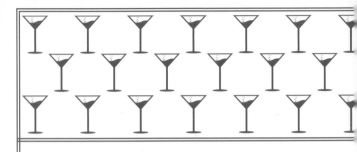

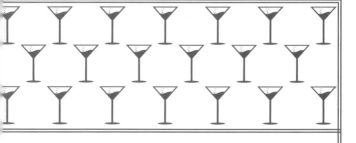

SHARERS &
PUNCHES

SEX ON THE BEACH

makes 3–4

2 measures vodka
2 measures peach schnapps
2 measures cranberry juice
2 measures orange juice
2 measures pineapple juice (optional)

To decorate
lemon wedges
lime wedges

Put 8–10 ice cubes into a cocktail shaker and add the vodka, schnapps, cranberry juice, orange juice and pineapple juice (if used).

Shake well.

Put 3–4 ice cubes into each highball glass, strain over the cocktail.

Decorate with lemon and lime wedges and serve.

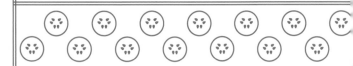

PINK
SANGRIA

3 measures rosé wine

2 teaspoons agave syrup

2 measures pomegranate juice

2 measures lemon verbena tea

2 measures soda water

pink grapefruit slice, to decorate

Pour the rosé wine into a glass, add 1 teaspoon of the agave syrup and stir until it dissolves.

Fill the glass up with ice cubes and add the remaining agave syrup, the pomegranate juice, lemon verbena tea and soda water.

Decorate with a slice of pink grapefruit and serve.

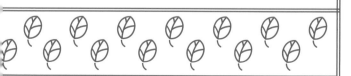

BLUSH SANGRIA

makes 1 large jug

4 measures vodka

2 measures crème de framboise

200 ml (7 fl oz) rosé wine

6 measures cranberry juice

2 measures lime juice

1 measure sugar syrup

6 measures soda water

edible flower petals, to decorate

Add all ingredients to a jug, then fill the jug with ice cubes.

Stir and decorate with edible flowers.

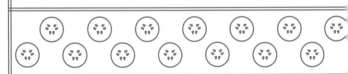

POPPIN'S GIN FIZZ

makes 4

4 measures gin

1½ agave syrup

250 ml (8 fl oz) sparkling wine

250ml (8 fl oz) hibiscus tea

4 measures pink grapefruit juice

raspberries, to decorate

Add the agave syrup and gin to a large jug and stir until the agave syrup dissolves.

Fill the jug with ice cubes and add the hibiscus tea, pink grapefruit juice and wine and stir.

Decorate with raspberries and serve.

TINTO DE VENEZIA

makes 1 large jug

4 measures Aperol
4 measures pink
grapefruit juice
4 measures orange juice
200 ml (7 fl oz) rosé wine
4 measures soda water

To decorate
orange slices
grapefruit slices

Fill a jug with ice cubes.

Add all the remaining
ingredients and stir.

Decorate with orange and
grapefruit slices and serve.

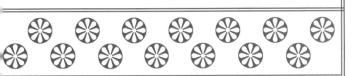

TORINO SPRITZER

makes 1 large jug

4 measures sweet vermouth
4 measures Campari
4 measures Triple Sec
4 measures lemon juice
200 ml (7 fl oz) lemon or
lime soda
200 ml (7 fl oz) red wine

To decorate
lemon slices
orange slices
grapefruit slices

Fill a jug with ice cubes.

Add all the remaining
ingredients to a jug and stir.

Decorate with lemon, orange
and grapefruit slices
and serve.

LA ROCHELLE PUNCH

makes 1 large jug

4 measures Cognac
50 g (2 oz) frozen mixed
berries, plus extra to serve
4 measures apple juice
2 measures lemon juice
2 measures sugar syrup
300 ml (½ pint) ginger ale

Add the Cognac and
berries to a food processor
or blender and blend until
smooth.

Pour into a jug.

Add plenty of ice cubes and
the remaining ingredients to
the jug and stir.

Decorate with berries and
serve.

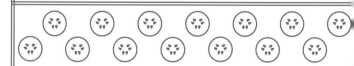

SHERRY
PUNCH

5 pineapple chunks
5 raspberries, plus extra
to decorate
3 lemon slices
2 measures fino sherry
2 teaspoons sugar syrup

To decorate
pineapple wedge
raspberry

Add the pineapple chunks,
raspberries, lemon slices
and sugar syrup to a cocktail
shaker and muddle.

Add the sherry and shake.

Strain into a glass full of
crushed ice, decorate with
a pineapple wedge and a
raspberry and serve.

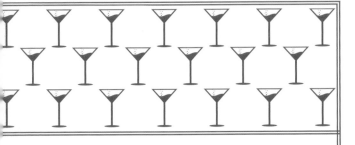

CHAMPAGNE
&
PROSECCO

BELLINI

½ ripe white peach
1 raspberry
2 teaspoons sugar syrup
5 measures prosecco, chilled

Put the peach, raspberry and sugar syrup into a food processor or blender and blend until smooth.

Strain into a flute glass, top with the prosecco and serve.

CHAMPINO

1 measure Campari
1¼ measures sweet vermouth
Champagne, to top up
lemon twist, to decorate

Pour the Campari and vermouth into a cocktail shaker and add some ice.

Shake, then strain into a chilled cocktail glass.

Top up with chilled Champagne and decorate with a lemon twist.

ROSSINI

4 strawberries
2 teaspoons sugar syrup
5 measures prosecco, chilled

Put the strawberries and sugar syrup into a food processor or blender and blend until smooth.

Strain into a flute glass, top with the prosecco and serve.

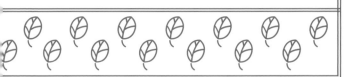

PARISIAN FIZZ

4 teaspoons raspberry purée

2 teaspoons passion fruit pulp

1 teaspoon sugar syrup

1 teaspoon pastis

4 measures chilled prosecco

raspberry, to decorate

Add all the indredients to a flute glass and stir.

Decorate with a raspberry and serve.

RIVIERA FIZZ

1½ measures sloe gin
½ measure fresh lemon juice
½ measure sugar syrup
Champagne, to top up
lemon twist, to decorate

Put the sloe gin, lemon juice and sugar syrup in a cocktail shaker with some ice and shake well.

Strain into a chilled champagne flute, top up with Champagne, stir and decorate with a lemon twist.

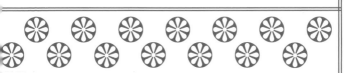

SBAGLIATO

1 measure Campari
1 measure sweet vermouth
2 measures prosecco
orange, to decorate

Add the ingredients to a rocks glass filled with cubed ice, stir briefly and decorate with a slice of orange.

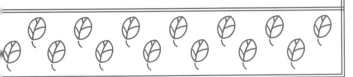

FRENCH 66

1 white sugar cube
6 dashes orange bitters
1 measure sloe gin
juice of ¼ lemon
chilled Champagne, to
top up
lemon twist, to decorate

Soak the sugar in the bitters then drop it into a champagne flute.

Add the sloe gin and lemon juice and stir.

Top up with chilled Champagne, decorate with a lemon twist.

BLACKWOOD BLUSH

2 measures grapefruit juice

2 measures rosé wine

2 teaspoons creme de mure

prosecco, to top

grapefruit and thyme, to decorate

Add all the ingredients except the prosecco to a wineglass filled with cubed ice.

Top with chilled prosecco, stir well and decorate with slice of grapefruit and a sprig of thyme.

COBBLER FIZZ

3 slices mandarin

2 raspberries, plus extra to decorate

2 teaspoons sugar syrup

1 measure fino sherry

4 measures prosecco, chilled

Add the mandarin, raspberries and sugar syrup to a cocktail shaker and muddle.

Add the sherry and shake.

Strain into a flute glass and top up with the prosecco.

Decorate with a raspberry and serve.

HEAD OVER HEELS

juice of 1 lime
1 teaspoon sugar syrup
2 measures vodka
3 drops Angostura bitters
pink Champagne, to top up
1 strawberry, to decorate

Put the ice cubes into a cocktail shaker.

Pour the lime juice, sugar syrup, vodka and Angostura over the ice and shake until a frost forms.

Pour without straining into a highball glass, top up with the Champagne, decorate with a strawberry.

ITALIAN DANDY

1 measure cognac
1 tsp cherry brandy
1 tsp sugar syrup
prosecco, to top
lemon twist, to decorate

Pour the cognac, cherry brandy and sugar syrup into a cocktail shaker or mixing glass filled with cubed ice.

Stir for 10 seconds and strain into a Champagne flute.

Top with chilled prosecco and decorate with a twist of lemon.

WATERMELON PUNCH

makes 1 large jug

3 measures vodka

1 measure strawberry liqueur

8 measures watermelon juice

2 measures lime juice

2 measures sugar syrup

1 x handful torn mint leaves

prosecco, to top

watermelon, mint & strawberry, to decorate

Add all the ingredients to a jug or punch bowl filled with cubed ice and stir well.

Decorate with slices of watermelon, whole strawberries and sprigs of mint.

PICTURE ACKNOWLEDGEMENTS

cover and interior icons:
Noun Project byarif fajar yulianto;
Marco Livolsi; Royyan Wijaya;
Thomas Bruck.

interior images:
123RF Jodie Johnson 43.
Octopus Publishing Group
Jonathan Kennedy 8, 19, 22, 27,
35, 54, 59, 60, 66, 69, 72, 75, 76,
82, 86, 91, 94; Stephen Conroy 13,
14, 28, 38, 48, 51, 65.